The American Poetry Series

BOXCARS

David Young

The Ecco Press New York

First published in 1973 by The Ecco Press
1 West 30 Street, New York, N.Y. 10001
Published simultaneously in Canada by
The Macmillan Company of Canada Limited
SBN 912-94606-7
Library of Congress catalog card number: 73-81357
Printed in U.S.A.
Designed by Ronald Gordon.

Acknowledgments
Some of these poems appeared first in the following magazines:
Antaeus, Colloquy, Lillabulero, Madrona, New American Review, New Republic, The Ohio Review, Poetry Northwest, and
Sumac; and in four anthologies: *Major Young Poets,* ed. Al Lee
(World), *Poetry Cleveland,* ed. Alberta Turner (Cleveland
State), *Just What the Country Needs, Another Poetry Anthology,*
ed. James McMichael and Dennis Saleh (Wadsworth), *The
Land on the Tip of a Hair,* ed. Wang Hui-Ming (Barre).

*For my sister Ruth
and my brother John*

Contents

BOXCARS

The Boxcar Poem

The boxcars drift by
clanking

they have their own
speech on scored
wood their own
calligraphy
Soo Line
they say in meadows
Lackawanna quick at crossings
Northern Pacific, a
nightmurmur, Northern
Pacific

even empty
they carry
in dark corners
among smells of wood and sacking
the brown wrappings of sorrow
the rank straw of revolution
the persistence of war

and often
as they roll past
like weathered obedient
angels you can see
right through them
to yourself
in a bright
field, a crow
on either shoulder.

Three for the Moon

1

A bluegreen January dusk
and the fullmoon
risen
          beyond the watertower

Leaving the office
suddenly foolish with joy
I have one thought:
we don't
deserve
this earth.

2

Tonight the moon is not an onion
above a yellow Spanish town

or a fresh cabbage
over a Russian village

tonight the moon has one name
and no figure but its own

though my arm is more than an arm
my briefcase a sleepy farm.

3

Say it is dawn in the mountains
after the shortest night of summer
and I kneel at a pool
still in the shadows
watching the last four stars
rock slightly
                    not winking out
but starting to join
the larger light

That is the feeling of the moon
as I drive home, flooding,
tumbling, part of the light
bright on the ice of the creek
round and fragrant in the pines

6

this watertower
looking glass
floodlight
moon!

Homing

1

"Attacks are being launched
to clean out enemy sanctuaries. . . ."

Watching the president's features
I'm childlike,
homesick.

For what?
A warm basement in Des Moines
a den in a thicket
the dense invisible pulsar
in the huge Crab Nebula. . . .

2

The visiting poet
has been on the bottle

all over Ohio. Come back
to the state he was born in,
missing his wife and New York apartment,
he rolls his big flushed
baby's head and whispers
"I want my mother."

Unwilling to be left alone
unwilling to talk to us
he recites for awhile like a bright child
and goes to bed hugging his misery.
Next morning he grabs a bus south.
I wave goodbye in the exhaust.
Everything's shaking.

3

The jackrabbit flushed by the car
is scared. In stiff
zigzag bounds he cuts
along the highway, then swerves suddenly
across an open field. Eighty yards to trees.
An easy shot.

But he knows
where he's going.

4

Pedaling home I glimpse
a seagreen boxcar
drifting along the tracks
by itself
and my uncle Bert, the best
farmer in the family
dressed in fresh overalls
clinging to the ladder
is he waving me off
or beckoning?

At dusk
a half dozen crows come
slowly over
the factory, the dairy
heading back
to their roost in the swamp

too far in
for hunters to follow.

In the yard
the smoke bush sings:
You have
nowhere to turn to
now.

5

Heavy and calm
summer rolls in
grass rises around us
like mother love
clouds build
in great treeshapes
yellow, peach, violet,
disperse or crash in storms
and the trees, cloudlike,
boil up in the wind
jittery, blazing green.

A black and yellow bird
—whose name escapes me—
startles me into pleasure
as I walk near the quarry
thinking of war, of the steady
state theory, of my children and
my parents, standing together
at Stonehenge
that Easter Sunday
my wife's mother
died of cancer.

Goldfinch! He flies up, wings
beating, is he in
my family, are we
home?

6

Sometimes I have to remember
to notice my children. Today
my daughter brought me a tulip
waxy and white, its petals

about to scatter—
hugging her I caught
in the fragrance of her hair
a smell of kinship.

Later we all
drove to the country
to see the green
sprouts in the long
plowed fields
the lambs, chickens, earthworms
who live so surely
on and in their earth, and when
we were tired
I glanced at the stacking clouds
and said
"Let's go home."

And we went
together, down the paved road,
and not
as each of us would go
sometime, alone,

rushing
across the black fields
toward the moon
that old bone
floating
out beyond evening.

May, 1970

In Heaven

There
where the self is a fine powder
drifting free

simply by wishing
you can be
whatever you like:
a fish swiped by a bear's paw
a woman whose son is insane
a spear in the side of a tiger

They do not feast there
they do not hymn perfection or
the ecstasies of love

for their own reasons
they care most
to assume the shapes of suffering:

helicopters swooning into clearings
through crossfire, burning

or an old hare
limping across
a stripped field
in late November.

The Owl

You know this dream. You move
down a moon road in a clouded
flower-heavy night; the
daylight terrors slumber:
missiles doze in their silos,
government fists uncurl, assassins
shelve their guns, the cops
sleep in their stink like bears,
Asians, Indians, Negroes,
cease their tunneling, the trucks
lie in the fields on their backs,
even the softball towns are stunned
and the farms gone back to grass.

Beautiful! All fireflies, buffalo
hills, a snow of love on the senses,
the tight labyrinths of time
turning to lowland mist, but
what is this owl come out of your head
to climb and hang, all talons and beak
two hundred yards overhead in the dark?
One thing is sure; he won't
slide in as easy as he got out,

he'll have to drop, hooks first,
into your stirring hair,
shatter and gouge his way
back to his perch . . .

The night quivers. After all
you are no more than a meal.
You stumble, arms out. The owl
begins his plunge. Now,
for the first time you hear
the celebrations in the distance:
bonfires you lit as a child
rabbits and savages, laughing, dancing.

To Die in a Tree

Silly. To die in a tree
on a smokeless winter day

held high like a sacrifice
or a shot coon, or a kite,

while the blood goes down
like sap, all afternoon,

watching fields jumble away
toward an ice-green sky

and darkness walking around
on the hard white pond.

Mandelstam

"He had difficulty breathing. . . . Osip breathed heavily; he was catching air with his lips."—Anna Akhmatova

1. *At the camp*

Hell freezing over. To keep sane
he studies the tiniest sensations
such as the touch of a necklace
of dry dead bees around a woman's neck.
Having said that, he can mention
honey, then speak of sunlight.
He studies his hands. Stalin's a swine.
Nadezhda's head is a beehive, full of poems.
He licks his lips to whisper one.
They're chapped. His breath is smoke.
His ears stick out, as if to catch
even the noise of a candleflame.
Frostbite will get them first.
A sledge goes past, stacked high.
Better not look. Ice lies in piles,
shoals, hummocks. Memories of Warsaw,
Paris, Petersburg, the warm Crimea,
keep their distance, Northern Lights,

or the swords of half-drunk cossacks
whirling through stupid dances.
He lives on garbage, is never warm, will die.

2. *The tear, 1938*

A tear is floating over Moscow
swollen, seeking a home, a mirror.

Tear, take my advice, get lost.
Those onion domes don't want you

the rivers are solid glass
the earth's a cake of permafrost

even those women wrapped in shawls
would gulp you like a drop of vodka.

Better go east, better follow
that long railway to Asia;

you can survive, little crystal,
in the glossy eye of a reindeer

on the bear's nose as he sleeps
dreaming sun into honey

in the fur of the wolf who runs
through the endless, falling snow.

3. *Nadezhda writes a letter*

Nonchalant, the sun goes off
and then returns. You won't.
Except in dreams, old films
flickering, buzzing when
your lips whisper, catching air,
making poems, soundtracks, and
I reach to touch you in the dark.

You left in a hurry, shrugging,
framed by policemen.
And your journey? The camps,
the cattlecars, beatings, stinks—
I see your forehead wrinkle, tongue thicken,
I turn away. Tears sting.
Maybe we should have jumped
hand in hand through the window!

It's warm in the Kremlin, there's music.
Stalin's small eyes glitter
his mustache is greasy with shashlik
he drinks, smashing his glass:
if the universe
makes any sense
how did we get from those fine-drawn
Petersburg afternoons
through the bonfires and rifleshots
of that marvelous revolution
to *this*?

But listen, Osip,
the joke's on them. Poems survive.
Your costly whispers carry.
They coexist with the state
like sunlight.
     I can
still hear you, Osip;
catching air, your highstrung voice
speaks for the frozen and forgotten
saying, it *was* their earth, it was
their earth. Purges don't change that!

Though that's dim comfort tonight
as I sit with my bread and soup
and the wind off the wrinkled plains
howls like a man without a tongue.
Brave man, who shredded the death warrants
of a leather-jacketed terrorist
and then ran wild through the Russian cold,
my warm sun, shrunk to a star,
it's a stiff, black world
you left behind.

Hearing You Read

for Stuart

that's a persuasive voice that makes
bread rise, slices it up and serves it
walks through each room of the embarrassed house
undaunted by domestic jumps, slaps, tears,
stiff sleepers, old windows, eggs, mirrors,
stands on a hill and interrupts the wind
using strings that snarl and entangle
to engineer reunions of the dead, the dying
the loved who were always hated, lesbian cooks
who made you notice sidewalks, czech refugees
who lied, pilots chewing their neckties, gloomy
fishermen, hunters sniffing their armpits, listen,
it's a rich soup where even the stones float up
while someone who came of age the hard way,
    descended
from sects who capered naked in the snow says gently
eat those they're good for you they're dumplings
swallow darling and close your eyes the walls
are buckling slowly from time's terrific

soft tornado and you're the type who'd drop
two tranquilizers and then count the bricks
stuart, the town is yours as well as this spilled
bucket of tennis balls don't stay up late
calm down rise up from the floor read on!

A Project for Freight Trains

Sitting at crossings and waiting for freights to pass, we have all noticed words—COTTON BELT / ERIE / BE SPECIFIC–SAY UNION PACIFIC / SOUTHERN SERVES THE SOUTH—going by. I propose to capitalize on this fact in the following way:

All freight cars that have high solid sides—boxcars, refrigerator cars, tank cars, hopper cars, cement cars —should be painted one of eight attractive colors, and have one large word printed on them:

1. Burnt orange freight cars with the word CLOUD in olive drab.
2. Peagreen freight cars with the word STAR in charcoal gray.
3. Rose-red freight cars with the word MEADOW in salmon pink.
4. Glossy black freight cars with the word STEAM in gold.
5. Peach-colored freight cars with the word AIR in royal blue.
6. Peach-colored freight cars with the word PORT in forest green.

7. Lavender freight cars with the word GRASS in vermilion or scarlet.
8. Swiss blue freight cars with the word RISING in chocolate brown.

When this has been accomplished, freight cars should continue to be used in the usual ways, so that the word and color combinations will be entirely random, and unpredictable poems will roll across the landscape.

Freight cars without words (i.e., without high or solid sides, such as flatcars, cattle cars, gondolas, automobile transporters, etc.) should all be painted white, to emphasize their function as spaces in the poems. Cabooses can be this color too, with a large black dot, the only punctuation.

Approximations of these random train poems can be arrived at by using the numbers above, plus 9 and 0 for spaces, and combining serial numbers from dollar bills, social security numbers, birthdates, and telephone numbers. The 5-6 combination, which makes

AIRPORT, is to be considered a lucky omen. 2-6 may be even luckier.

This project would need to be carried out over the entire United States at once. Every five years a competition could be held among poets to see who can provide the best set of colors and words for the next time.

The Accident

The poem walks through a drizzle
wearing overalls. It loads

big Nouns in a pickup truck
climbs in the cab, guns the

motor and is off, knuckles white,
peering at silence   among trees

past smoking fields   blue meadows
over bridges of electric air

to unmarked crossings where the long
trains of the past come through

with the momentum of all their stations
and the truck must be hit

exploding in every direction
while the poem somehow survives

in the circle of wreckage and rain
where the X has begun to spin.

Poem for Wrists

Wrists! I want to
write you a poem you
whom nurses finger watches
circle razors open
handcuffs chill—you are
taken for granted wrists!
therefore assert yourselves
take charge of your
unruly friends the hands
keep them from triggers, off
necks give them a light
touch have them wave bye-bye
teach them to let
go at the right moment oh
wrists shy ankles of the arm
on whom farms flyrods
shovels whips and poems
so naturally depend.

Thoughts of Chairman Mao

1

Holding black whips
the rulers rode
in the blue hills.

But the peasants were everywhere and nowhere,
a soft avalanche, gathering
courage; in famines
we ate the mules, tasting vinegar,
lived among rocks above the passes,
and gradually became an army
red flags snapping in the wind
and I wrote of "a forest of rifles,"
and of heroes strolling home
against a smoky
sunset.

2

Wars merge like seasons;
sometimes over hot wine
the old campaigners try to remember
who we were fighting that winter

on this plateau, that plain,
and whether we won.

It blurs . . .
miles in boxcars
doors wedged open
miles across blue-shadowed snow.
Hungry evening.

Artillery at the river
bodies in the rice fields
a black truck on its side
burning . . .

At night we could hear the gibbons
calling each other up the valley.
When there was a rest or a vista
someone would write a poem.
It blends and blurs:
conferences melonseeds sabotage
dungfires treaties mosquitoes
my great red army on the march
blinking in the sunshine.

3

Now it is changed.
I am the giant in the pageant,
toothy, androgynous, quilted.

To the slow roll of drums
my effigy speaks to the people
of harvests, steelmills, stars.

In the puppetshows I battle
enemies of the state
sometimes with blows and curses
sometimes with love and flowers
while Marx pops up to hug me
and Lenin takes my arm.

I would have done it
with poems! Instead
I have come to be
a red book, a pumped-up myth,
from Long March to Big Swim
surfacing, always surfacing:

said to have gone
miles through golden water
wrestled the Yangtze and won,
water god, flower king, rice prince;

the current takes me on
and it is no small thing
riding these tides, wave upon
wave of love, smiling, unspeaking,
ten thousand miles of mountains and water,
a chanting race, a skin on history,

until the people rise and go,
dispersing me.

4

At the end I enter a small room.

Stalin is standing there alone

hands behind his back
gazing out the window.

We link arms. We merge.

And the rulers ride the blue hills
holding their black whips high.

Ohio

Looking across a field
at a stand of trees
—more than a windbreak
less than a forest—
is pretty much all
the view we have

in summer it's lush
in winter it gets
down to two or
three tones   for
variety
there might be
an unpainted barn
water patches
a transmission tower

yet there's a lot
to see
        you could sit
all day on the rusty
seat of a harrow
with that view before you

and all the sorrows
this earth has seen
sees now   will see
could pass through
you like a long
mad bolt of lightning
leaving you drained
and shaken
still
at dusk
the field would be
the same and the growing
shadows of the trees
would cross it toward you
until you rose   your heart
pounding with joy and walked
gladly through the weeds
and toward the trees

February

1

The plow comes on.
Two lights inside a huge
white wave of snow.

2

The balloon we made
of garbage bags
yaws in the wind,
will not ascend.

What's the right song?
"Unhand that panda!"

3

Now the river, trembling a little.
Turtle oil.

4

Said he had a weasel
in the sack. Black nuts.

Logs, a spritz of yellow weeds.
Crow tracks. Arrows.

5

Double sunlight. A child
trots in a circle in the snow.
One cardinal, bright as a wound,
sails from a spruce to a bush.
Even when happiness
rises through your body
terrible sorrows
are an inch from either cheek.
Can you go on? Listen:
this book the earth
is turning a page.

Love Song
for Chloe

I guess your beauty doesn't
bother you, you wear it easy
and walk across the driveway
so casual and right it makes
my heart weigh twenty pounds
as I back out and wave
thinking She's my summer
peaches, corn, long moondawn dusks
watermelons chilling in a tub
of ice and water: mirrored there
the great midsummer sky
rolling with clouds and treetops
and down by the lake
the wild canaries
swinging on the horse mint
all morning long.

The Cutting Room Floor

You had your life
shot on location

Now you lean back in the dark
humming softly and smiling

But where are the best shots?
the bone face that rose among trees
the fast river in the empty park
where snow fell, covering the baby
the President and his assistant
struggling in the swimming pool
the distant banjos on the soundtrack
that rabbit black against the sky
and the effigy, dancing alone
at night in the wet meadow . . .

Back there
on the cutting room floor

The Courier's Lost Memoirs

sponging the Czar's face as he lay in fever
the suitcase resembling a drum
butterfly net at the ready
all the dark squadrons weeping
where the cruiser lay on the veldt
helpless and steaming

carrying paintings into the burning manor
the frozen carriage of the Swedish count
surrounded by murmuring peasants
mineral pastilles for the tonsils
the seaside resorts of Australia
"ten guineas," coughing, "in a little box"

men from the Balkans huddled in the doorways
macassar oil in their whiskers
near the family mourning warehouse
overdressed children watching
cavalry on bicycles and the strange trip
up the Mt. Pilatus railway near Lucerne

"perfect obedience to superiors"
said the Queen, her cheeks shaking
Portuguese colonies in sunlight
the Irish channel seething
the girls of Provence, easily seduced
and California lying golden on its fault

Chromos

1

Why have I pinned this postcard up?

> Orange flames lick
> the volcano's purple rim
> under a plum-blue sky.

Wow.
I picture your face and breasts
lit by that glow. I decide
we will visit Hawaii.

2

> Like a strange church the jet
> sits in silhouette
> under a dark grape dawn.

The runway looks deserted;
maybe the pilot, yawning,
is climbing into his harness.

At the horizon a wild
incandescence, yellow-white

as if the world was starting to burn.

3

In a slate-green night the lighthouse
pokes its beam at a right
angle to itself.

The beam looks solid
a dowel, a tube
a flattering self-portrait
of the lighthouse.

4

The sky is navy blue
the Flatiron Building's a handsome
reddish-brown, speckled
with tiny yellow squares.

A lemon on a divan, the moon
watches from puffy clouds
thinking trout? basket? lightship?

5

What I want to do
is fan out a handful
of new cards, dazzlers.
Take a card:

> Geysers of light
> that mate around cities

> Mountains waxed and polished

> A picture of the well
> in the bottom of the sky

> The gears of light toward which
> we fall so gently as they knit

> The blades, teardrops, sphincters
> of lampshine

47

It's our appetite for light, it's how
the world keeps pushing back
the world we must invent,
all that give and take . . .
Take a card:

>   Those places I hoped to live:
>   the Residence of Dorothy Lamour,
>   Ethel Farley's Inn, the Willow
>   Banks Hotel, and most of all,
>   the Golden Temple of Jehol,
>   are ablaze, blooming, collapsing . . .

By their light I can just
make out this postcard
this chromolithograph
this poem.

Notes on the Poems

1 Was found in an orchard;
  is three or four thousand years old;
  was probably made with poor tools
  by the light of an oil lamp throwing
  shadows against the wall
  that would frighten us now.

2 Would never have been possible without
  that famous fog of December 9th
  for out of that fog came Geraldine
  wearing a dress of chipmunk furze
  with a grackle perched on her wrist.

3 Whole families were involved here
  and the death wish and the industrial
  revolution. You say the third line
  about the bathroom in the grocery
  was troublesome; I ask,
  should a poem make more sense than Omaha?

4 It is right, little poem about
  wandering and misunderstanding
  that you kept coming back, unwanted.

Small avalanche,
always missing your victims,
come here—
I open my arms.

5 Of course the opening stanza
   is like a cheap decal
   of roses and tulips
   on the side of a laundry hamper.
   But as the poem progresses
   you see something crawling
   from one of the flowers.
   An insect? Bend closer.
   It is a very small man, holding a flashlight.
   He snaps it on and swings the beam toward you.
   You are blinded.

The Death of the Novel

1

As she shook her little fist
her filmy gown
swung open.
"*Sacre bleu!*" he gasped.
"Shall we seal this pact
as only a man and woman can?"

Outside the jungle chattered in the dawn.

2

Claude paused to wipe his brow.
The tractor sputtered, idling;
a cow stared from a nearby field.

What had his father meant?
How would he ever get
to college? It
all seemed out of joint, and yet . . .

3

Because he took her everywhere
in his old droshky, they made a stir
in all the villages that summer
while she grew to like, then to adore
his very pawkiness, his air
of staggering kindness. Love flared,
kindling her cheeks. She picked a flower.

4

And now the glade
where Stan was sprawled
grew still. A bird
twittered, insects drowsed.

And then
a shrill scream came
from the middle distance,
came again, and Stan's
heart jumped. The noon
express! Would Anne, or Kim,
be on that train?

5

Bertram rattled the door, a wild
glare on his face, teeth clenched:
"What have you done with my manuscript?"
The undertaker smiled.

The Monuments of Egypt

Vincent had written a tiny modern classic.
He was showing it to Luigi, his childhood
Chum and long-standing
Squash partner. "Don't
Drop it, Luigi," he cautioned,
"It's tiny and fragile and there are no copies
Yet!"
          "Vincent" —Luigi spoke carefully—
"You've written a tiny
Modern classic here!" Vincent looked half
Convinced; he examined the handle
Of his squash racquet modestly.

"What bothers me," Luigi went on,
"Is that you never sent it to my magazine
Which, as you know, is foremost
In these things. All we seem to get
Are pale young imitations of your work
By pale young men. Mmmmmm?"

Vincent squirmed. What was
The source of his discomfort?

And why had he not sent a single
Modern classic to Luigi?

Was it procrastination? Was it his habit
Of going to Europe whenever Luigi was going
To Press? Or was it some darker
Motive, stored away in the nether
Part of his psyche, as a jar of potatoes
Is stored in a cool brown cellar?

Having to do perhaps with squash,
Or with his unconscious suspicion that this
Luigi was not his childhood chum at all, but a
Different and stranger Luigi, a rascal,
A smasher of tiny modern classics . . .

"Give it back," he said desperately,
"Give it back, give it back!"

A Country Postcard

September here, a haze on things,
diamond mornings, dying corn.
We have green fields here, white-flecked,
we have blue fields here, chicory,
yellow fields, four kinds of goldenrod,
and a man in a white shirt
and a red face
a man made out of words
stands by the B & O tracks
listening for the express
that disappeared west
before the tracks
began to rust.

There's a stillness
this morning, that the man
made out of words must walk through
listening
as he wades

in chicory, alfalfa,
wild carrot, goldenrod,
the nodding, growing
dew-decked, soon-to-die
words.

A Calendar: The Beautiful Names
of the Months

January

On this yearly journey two
faces are better—a weary
woman, a wary man.

February

Where the earth goes
to run a fever. The care's good.
Herbs brew. The rooms are airy.

March

Bridge curving over a swamp.
A bruise that smarts, the long
patience of an army.

April

Neither grape nor apple.
Any monkey, a pearly sprig,
a prism. Flute notes.

May

The arch opens. Crowds.
Goats, babies, vowels and
the wind, permitting anything.

June

A jury rises.
The moons of Jupiter
set. Bugs, berries, prairie grass.

July

Jewelers snooze on the grass,
one eye open for the tall
constellation-poppies.

August

Clearing your throat of dust.
Wading in lagoons . . . algae,
hot bursts of wind.

September

Lives away from his brothers,
gentle-tempered, a little solemn.
Bears pests, eats peas and beets.

October

Cold roots and a fresh-caught owl
rocked on a cot.
An orange boot.

November

Toothache and memory.
Nine women. Overdressed beavers.
No new members.

December

Something decent, easy.
Frozen meekness. Wax. A good
end, an ember, then ten of them.

60

The Big Blue Water Tower

It stands on the east
edge of town rising through
brown trees just
behind the Chrysler
Plymouth dealer
                    the moon
rises beyond it
and the sun
this huge metal
baby blue
sphere on stilts

Do water towers walk
the fields by night
and meet   and mate?

Maybe not maybe
there are no spells
to make them dance
bring rain bless
families but

if I were a crow
I'd do what that one
is doing this dim
winter noon
I'd circle
slowly upward from
the ground sketching
its size   its shape
my homage to
this blue master
water tower
color of
the air

The Middle of December

At sunset the shadow of the oak
walked across the creek
into the second growth

These winter
evenings! The light
rose in a slow silence as
the dark grew below
                         Now
it's midnight, it's
my thirty-third birthday, I walk out
to watch a quiet frost
grow in the starlight

Thirty-three years
finding this lit
world enough
I've mostly been
a happy man
an oak, an owl, a fool

Struck by that
I laugh
watching my white
breath   rise
          bloom   drift off

"It's a Whole World, the Body.
A Whole World!"
—*Swami Satchidananda*

1

No, it's a tenement.
You enter from the top,
feeling your way down the bad stairs,
sniffing.

Someone is practicing
on a rubber piano
in the elbow.

Gangsters in the stomach,
splitting their loot.

These peeling walls, these puddles,
babies screaming in the back,
shoulder arguing with neck.

There's a big party in the groin;
you aren't invited.

2

Or it's open country.
Steady rivers, muscular pastures,
deep weeds, foothills.

Nobody lives off
the fat of the land.

Huge clouds come up without warning:
brainstorms.

3

Say it's an ocean.
Ladies wade there, shuddering.
Surgeons pass in their yachts.

Hiccup: a message
in a bottle.

The pervert descends
in his submarine.

4

Swami, the body's a butcher shop,
a family lost in a wax museum,
moonless planet, ancient civilization,
a swami, a world,
seldom whole.

At the Back of the Year in a High Wind

winter

the sun crawls through a sewer pipe

the moon that silver truck
drives off through shaking trees

little shrubs that edge potato fields
are wringing their hands saying We
were not meant to be adventurous

and here comes a prairie chicken
tumbling over and over
                              she has come
a long way
                from the west

and is going a long way

to the conventions of the clouds
the master classes of the snow

Pelee Island, Lake Erie

for Carol and Dewey Ganzel

It's a fine line
between what was abandoned
and what was never settled

but this island
where the wheat looks out of place
a dying man sells corn
and scarecrows sound like shotguns

is the right place to knock
foreheads with nature
and grow accustomed
to the idea of perishing:

the lake shifts carefully on its bed
flies herd us toward the water
the fish decay, leaving precious tokens

and a light shines behind our skins
making us useful
                        like beacons
and giving us when we stroll
through beach litter and driftwood
a knack for making shadows

Teddy Roosevelt

stumping again it hurts by god
have travelled all around the tattooed
lady my country looking for the right
spot to raise the banner of straw some
watertower some windmill though my big head
aches and i miss the wax works greatly
clouds hang above old toads strange poppies
acetylene evenings seven fireflies solitude
blue pastures where a bull paws up cool soil
dragging my bad leg through the spirit village
seized by the women covered with sycamore leaves
as if i was the corn dog the potato man
no one knows me understands my language
the pulse of the tattooed lady is bad
i fear for her life i fear for her death
i would give her both if i could but i sit
here on the porch of this rainsmoke penthouse
while the music rises like mosquito smudge
through which a red sun comes rolling rolling

Woodrow Wilson

I pull on the tight clothes and go walking
rectitude misting around my figure
carrying the book of shadows a low moon
crosses the powerstations the refineries
and in the needle mountains there are lakes
so cold and clear that the dead who sit
at the bottom in buggies and machinegun nests
look up past the trout who nibble their shoulders
to see the eclipse begin the dime-sized shadow
sliding across the sun the insects settling
around the bears in their yokes the antelopes
acting out all their desires old lady
who smothers her young in her iron robes
you have wrung my thin neck a thousand times
and taken my pinchnose glasses but
I come back again with the gliding indians
settlers who have forgiven all their tools
the shabby buffaloes wild sheep wapiti
the inland sea that looks at the sky all day
with only a widgeon's wake to disturb it
the V dividing away from itself
all night under trembling constellations

Water Diary

walking the tracks in early March
thinking where would I store a handcar
we ponder the fast clouds my son and I
and stare at winter's house   look down:
smashed grass gravel in a pool rainrings
wet rust on the tracks the creek rushing
no trains today no setting out arriving
the wind bucketing off through the trees
and sunset a skin of ice on each red puddle

my eyes heavy   the plumtree burning
muscles in my neck twist and I
reach toward you   even in summer air
your face is cool   a winter window
steelwork   we drive off the city lies
in haze behind but this
hot mist is everywhere
unsketching the little towns
and the fields with their cows and flies

the punt bumps the bank
jump ashore kick the boat back
to circle in the current
the black cinders crunch
here's the cottage the old man
sleeps at his desk everything's
familiar the blue door the sweater
over a chair the picture of a glacier
the ginger beer the luger on the rug
the wind breathing in the fireplace
wells cisterns rainwater
lady lady lady lady

the ocean in its shirtsleeves humming
while we mull over a Spanish poem
called either "Angel Horse" or "Autumn Spit"

bump bump a kind of knife and spotted rocks
the forest lily stands up straight
never making a stain you enter the water

sugar the waves around the cliffs
and the walker pausing in plimsolls
the cold arm reaching down the lobster

and the house across the cove
browns in the sunlight the sea lion
dripping and watching the tipped boats the islands

o stiff cadets your buttons shine
the rows of corn the aimed November wind
ran over a black snake near the quarry
going the wrong direction the daylight
racing across the clouds the dusty city
where a whole brass band got lost on purpose
or the sky where long blue moving vans
park to study aviation and the stars
what do you know about river currents
wheat sperm fountain lions drill towers
what it means to be human stop it at once

huge rock bouncing down the mountain
snapping pine trees striking sparks
smashed that fragrant berrypatch
it's not a rock it's a word the word 'rose'
it destroyed my cabin narrowly missing the hammock
now it's growing smaller it's the size
of a panel truck a plow horse a rowboat
an easy chair an unabridged dictionary
a telephone a brick a baby's rattle
an aspirin and now
it falls in a puddle and disappears
while I write "the wordboulder, a rose,
bounced into the lake and sank. . . ."

these lemons are packed in ice
then shipped to skating rinks in the Dakotas
or imagine a river of very chilly whiskey
lumber barons along the banks
we have all seen helicopters flying sideways
data processing centers in Tennessee
astrakhan collars rain pocking snow
every direction is good and today
it has something to do with the cedar waxwing
seen at the feeder while I read Shakespeare
like starting over in the arms of water
"your body finds naturally its liberty"

the Empress seized the throne by unsavory means
and the poets strolled morose in the cashew orchards
young men were ridiculed by the thistle gate
while purple swallows flew in the snowy foothills
it is all the same   time   all the same
"Who now remembers," mused the Secretary of Rituals
"the monkey chariots that drew the courtesans
among the jade fountains and the pruned bamboo?"
and as he spoke, gazing out at his pepper plants
the invention of movable type occurred
and the waters of immortality faded from view

on the threshold my eyes go bang
I have fulfilled potatoes dealt justly with salt
allowed to stand the dyer's hand but a rough
irresponsible manner with ladies at parties
and the tongue was king the air fumetti
the ego bathing in the cataract thought
even the branches seemed to be nodding assent
but I did it wrong I know I did it's the
empty paper nest of the stupid wasps
the puzzle that needs to be swept off the table
the train rolling round its tin circle of track
my grandfather smiling and watching

the olive-colored water spoke again
'49 Packards drew up to the Turkey Shoot
The Autobiography of Honolulu   listen
the water spoke volumes and the fruit
carved by the light of mutton tallow
made a perfectly good prize for the best
drop of water sliding down the cheek
imagine all this as a sort of waterclock
though not the kind that drips or burns
rising the months rising the mist rising
the spirits rising the mountains rising
meadowlarks constellations words

bruised the words getting them into place
thought of the sea lifting its knees
steadily thought of the elbows of plants
rusty cans daisy fleabane yellowstone canyon
it's cold in history and colder still
in the imagination or this wide plowed field
where you stand in a thick snowstorm roaring
your whole body going up in flames or do you
stare through a window at a passing truck
on which there's a picture of a burning man
shaking his fists in a blizzard

water is beads on the eaves steam
from a manhole cover most of my body
tears saliva urine sweat meadows flooding
what the spinning windmill pumps what
rains and bounces on mountainslopes
sinks into darkening earth is lost
and found again in giant summer clouds
shapechanger fog where glacier meets ocean
yesterday dew all over the freightcar
rimefrost today swamp pools tomorrow
imagination colorless and holding every color
window and mirror holding any image
the green creek wrinkling with a mallard
settling toward its own reflection in the sky
is time as line as circle is the snowman sinking
back inside himself is what can't be named is water

wrinkle wrinkle movie star the ice bird sang
she put her marvelous foot on the next step down
and shock waves traveled the length of her body
at the banquet there was a swan carved out of ice
and several people dreamed of riding it naked
into that distance where light is no longer king
and nothing moves in the endless black lagoons
but darkness itself with a faint and dangerous slopping

for several days the temperature stood so low
that at last we could walk on water   and we did
the creek creaked softly talking to itself
along the banks through harmless fissures
we brushed some snow aside and peered down through
but could see nothing not water not even ourselves
there was a strange sensation of wrinkles and darkness
we knocked on the stuff   for entrance   for luck
and an old man spoke from a book
"why can't mind and matter
be more like wind and water?"
we looked up   snow was wobbling toward us
through miles and miles and miles of soundless air